JESUS WROTE THE

TEN (10)

COMMANDMENTS.

(HE ABOLISHED NONE AT CALVARY)

METUSELA F. ALBERT

To order additional copies of this book, contact:
Xlibris
844-714-8691
www.Xlibris.com
Orders@Xlibris.com

ISBN: Softcover   978-1-6641-5282-3
        EBook   978-1-6641-5283-0

Library of Congress Control Number: 2021901309

Print information available on the last page.

Rev. date: 01/20/2021

Contents

INTRODUCTION

Welcome to another episode. The fact that you bought this book and want to read it, proves that you do not want to be deceived any further like the others. So, stay tuned and be prepared to make some changes to your beliefs, if you are one that has been taught or believed that JESUS changed the Ten Commandments at Calvary when he died.

Christianity has been bombarded with so much lies for so long by those wolves clothed in sheep's clothing and they no longer know what is truth from error. It is time that we as professed Christians who like to hear and obey the truth in Jesus, take our stand against the churches (denominations) and pastors who preached the cheap grace doctrines about JESUS without his Ten Commandments.

Believe it or not? Most professed Christians, Pastors, and mainline mega Churches believed that JESUS abolished the Ten Commandments at Calvary. What a shame!

So what?

Are they free to commit adultery now since the Ten Commandments were abolished at Calvary, as they claimed? . . . Are they free to kill someone and not become responsible for the crime? Aren't they contradicting themselves? Of course, they are. They don't even know their own contradiction.

In fact, a vast majority of them don't even know that JESUS was the Almighty God of Abraham who created the heaven and the earth in six literal days. He was the Almighty God of Abraham who wrote the Ten Commandments on Mount Sinai on two tablets of stone and gave through Moses for all mankind, Jew or Gentile, circumcised or uncircumcised, male or female, black, red, brown, yellow, or white.

JESUS was the everlasting God the Father of the Old and New Testaments who humbly took up the role of the Son of God in human flesh in the New Testament. He said, "If you love **me**, keep **my** commandments." (John 14:15). JESUS also said, "Before Abraham was, I am." (John 8:58).

Dear folks, fasten your seat belts and get ready for the take off. If you need two or three seat belts, please do so because there will be some turbulence, pumps, and shaking along the way before we safely land at our final destination.

This book is not another book to display and decorate your bookshelf for ego status. It will blast your mind to pieces and you will not believe again in <u>the false doctrine</u> that says – JESUS changed the Ten Commandments at Calvary after his death.

Therefore, you will not believe again in the heresy that says – Jesus changed the Sabbath commandment and now Sunday is the Sabbath day.

. . . .

Below is a brief timeline of Biblical history to help us understand the great events and characters mentioned in the Bible.

. . . .

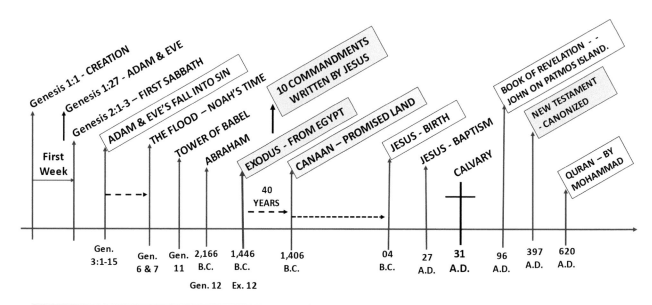

NOTE: Three months after the children of Israel left Egypt, God (YAHWEH) spoke the Ten Commandments and wrote them on two tablets of stone and gave through Moses on Mount Sinai. This event took place around 1,446 B.C. as per the timeline chart shown above – (Exodus 12-20; 31:18).

This is an important timeline chart that needs to be understood by the student of the Bible and all Pastors.

JESUS was that YAHWEH who spoke the Ten Commandments. HE wrote the Ten Commandments.

. . . .

CHAPTER 1

THERE ARE TEN (10) COMMANDMENTS, NOT NINE (9) COMMANDMENTS.

1. Where can we find and read the Ten Commandments in the Bible?

You can turn your Bible to Exodus 20:1-17, and read them in there.

Exodus 20:1-17 (KJV).

20 And God spake all these words, saying,

² **I am the LORD thy God, which have brought thee out of the land of Egypt, out of the house of bondage.**

³ **Thou shalt have no other gods before me.**

⁴ **Thou shalt not make unto thee any graven image, or any likeness of any thing that is in heaven above, or that is in the earth beneath, or that is in the water under the earth.**

⁵ **Thou shalt not bow down thyself to them, nor serve them: for I the LORD thy God am a jealous God, visiting the iniquity of the fathers upon the children unto the third and fourth generation of them that hate me;**

⁶ **And shewing mercy unto thousands of them that love me, and keep my commandments.**

⁷ **Thou shalt not take the name of the LORD thy God in vain; for the LORD will not hold him guiltless that taketh his name in vain.**

⁸ **Remember the sabbath day, to keep it holy.**

⁹ **Six days shalt thou labour, and do all thy work:**

¹⁰ **But the seventh day is the sabbath of the LORD thy God: in it thou shalt not do any work, thou,**

nor thy son, nor thy daughter, thy manservant, nor thy maidservant, nor thy cattle, nor thy stranger that is within thy gates:

[11] **For in six days the LORD made heaven and earth, the sea, and all that in them is, and rested the seventh day: wherefore the Lord blessed the sabbath day, and hallowed it.**

[12] Honour thy father and thy mother: that thy days may be long upon the land which the LORD thy God giveth thee.

[13] Thou shalt not kill.

[14] Thou shalt not commit adultery.

[15] Thou shalt not steal.

[16] Thou shalt not bear false witness against thy neighbor.

[17] Thou shalt not covet thy neighbor's house, thou shalt not covet thy neighbor's wife, nor his manservant, nor his maidservant, nor his ox, nor his ass, nor any thing that is thy neighbor's.

. . . .

EXPLANATION

THE SPOKEN TEN COMMANDMENTS – Exodus 20:1-17.

In Exodus chapter 19, the children of Israel were commanded to sanctify themselves for 3 days and not to come so close to Mount Sinai when God speaks to them. Whosoever touches the Mountain will surely die. A holy God will speak to them about his holy law.

In Exodus Chapter 20:1-17, God spoke the Ten Commandments to the children of Israel while they were camping at the foot of Mt. Sinai after leaving Egypt. It took them about three months of travelling from Egypt to this point at Mount Sinai.

Before reaching Mount Sinai, the children of Israel were given manna to eat. The manna did **not** fall on the Sabbath day **(Exodus 16)**. A great miracle about the manna on the seventh day. When they kept the left-over manna on any other day of the week, it goes bad the next day. But on Friday, the manna is kept till the Sabbath day and yet did **not** go bad. What an amazing miracle!

WHAT IS THE POINT?

The children of Israel knew of the Sabbath day before they reached Mount Sinai where God wrote the Ten Commandments on two tablets of stone – (Exodus 31:18).

Therefore, the Sabbath Commandment was not for the Jews only, but for all generations.

Actually, the Ten Commandments were not a new law to the children of Israel. Their forefathers beginning from Abraham were aware of it. But after about 430 years in slavery in Egypt in a foreign land with heathen gods, the descendants of Abraham, Isaac, and Jacob had forgotten their one God and his Commandments. And many of them worshiped the idol gods of the Egyptians.

Thus, **God (YAHWEH)** had to remind them that he alone was the only God who brought them out of slavery in Egypt; and they were not to worship any other gods nor make any images in his name.

. . . .

THE WRITTEN TEN COMMANDMENTS – Exodus 31

CATCH THIS: The Ten Commandments are God's moral law. It is NOT the law of Moses. When you failed to understand this truth, then you will fall into Satan's prey like most professed Christians who speak, teach, preach that JESUS abolished the Ten Commandments at Calvary after his death.

REMEMBER THIS AND NOT TO FORGET.

Moses did <u>**not**</u> write the Ten Commandments. And the Ten Commandments were not given for the Jews but through Moses for ALL mankind, Jew and Gentile, circumcised and non-circumcised.

THE TEN COMMANDMENTS ARE NOT THE LAW OF MOSES.

The Ten Commandments are God's moral law, the law of liberty. This is <u>**not**</u> the health law nor the civil law.

There are Ten (10) Commandments, not nine (9) Commandments. So, stop making the Sabbath Commandment as if it is not part of the Ten Commandments. Stop separating the Sabbath Commandment from the other nine Commandments.

Dear Christian friends, stop separating the Sabbath Commandment from JESUS who is the LORD of the Sabbath day.

Those who have an ear, please listen carefully and stop rejecting JESUS and His law. You cannot separate JESUS from His Ten Commandments. His law is holy and righteous – (Romans 7:12).

ALL MANKIND WILL BE JUDGED BY THE MORAL LAW (THE TEN COMMANDMENTS) –

SCRIPTURE: Ecclesiastes 12:13-14.

"Let us hear the conclusion of the whole matter: Fear God and keep his commandments: for this is the whole duty of man. For God shall bring every work into judgment, with every secret thing, whether it be good, or whether it be evil."

. . . .

WE WILL BE JUDGED BY THE TEN COMMANDMENTS

• Ecclesiastes 12 :13 -14 .

• "Let us hear the conclusion of the whole matter : Fear God and keep his commandments : for this is the whole duty of man . For God shall bring every work into judgment, with every secret thing, whether it be good, or whether it be evil ."

CHAPTER 2

JESUS WAS ABRAHAM'S GOD. HE WROTE THE TEN COMMANDMENTS.

SCRIPTURE - Exodus 20:1-5

1. And God spake all these words, saying,

² **I am the LORD thy God, which have brought thee out of the land of Egypt, out of the house of bondage.**

³ **Thou shalt have no other gods before me.**

⁴ Thou shalt not make unto thee any graven image, or any likeness of anything that is in heaven above, or that is in the earth beneath, or that is in the water under the earth.

⁵ Thou shalt not bow down thyself to them, nor serve them: for I the LORD thy God am a jealous God, visiting the iniquity of the fathers upon the children unto the third and fourth generation of them that hate me;

. . . .

EXPLANATION

The same God (YAHWEH) who spoke to Moses at the burning bush called – "I AM THAT I AM" was the God who wrote the Ten Commandments.

In the New Testament, JESUS said, "Before Abraham was, I AM." (John 8:58).

It is clear that JESUS was the God (YAHWEH) who spoke to Moses at the burning bush. He was the God who wrote the Ten Commandments on two tablets of stone – (Exodus 31:18). He was the Almighty God of Abraham, Isaac, and Jacob.

JESUS alone is God. There is no other god besides him – (Isaiah 44:6, 24; 45:1-7, 21-22). He alone is the Savior. There is no other Savior.

THE FIRST FOUR COMMANDMENTS OF THE TEN COMMANDMENTS –

When we truly love God, we would love to keep his first four Commandments. The first four commandments are summed up in one commandment – LOVE THE LORD YOUR GOD WITH ALL YOUR HEART.

THE LAST SIX COMMANDMENTS OF THE TEN COMMANDMENTS –

If we truly love God, we would also love our neighbor. Therefore, the last six commandments are summed up in one commandment called – LOVE YOUR NEIGHBOR AS THYSELF.

When you love your God and your neighbor, you will not want to commit adultery with your neighbor's wife or husband.

When you sin against your neighbor, you are sinning against your God which is JESUS who created us.

. . . .

CHAPTER 3

SIN IS THE TRANSGRESSION OF GOD'S COMMANDMENTS.

Scripture:

1 John 3:4 (KJV).

[4] Whosoever committeth sin transgresseth also the law: <u>for sin is the transgression of the law.</u>

. . . .

EXPLANATION

1. **The law has to be transgressed in order for anyone to become a sinner.**

2. **No person can become a sinner except by the transgression of God's law.**

3. **No baby in the mother's womb is a sinner because the baby cannot transgress God's law.**

4. **Sin is not something that can be transferred or inherited from another person.**

5. **Sin is not something that can be inherited from whosoever, let alone from Adam.**

6. **Sin is by a decision, a choice by an individual person who knows good from evil.**

7. **Sin is not by your place of birth or color or gender.**

8. **Sin is not by nature nor by Adam's sin.**

9. **No baby conceived in the mother's womb is a sinner.**

10. **No baby knows good and evil in the mother's womb.**

11. **No baby can repent of any sin, and that is the reason no baby is a sinner in the mothers' womb.**

. . . .

When the above 11 points are understood well, then you as a creature, wonderfully created by a loving God, know very well that He did not create you in the image of the devil, a sinner.
A loving God never created you a murderer nor an adulterer nor a prostitute nor an idol worshiper, etc. You were not born a sinner from Adam's sin. Period!

If you failed to reason this carefully, then you have a problem of illogical thinking to make God as the Creator of baby sinners from Adam. Therefore, you have made God as the one who created you a baby sinner, a killer, a robber, an adulterer, a fornicator, a prostitute, etc.

Therefore, you have an excuse to sin forever while you are alive. Apparently, you have immortalized sin for every baby. Thus, you have rejected the atonement of JESUS at Calvary as our Sin Bearer. Therefore, you have made all babies born to this earth become the Sin Bearer for Adam and Eve.

Because of your false theory, you have become a thread to our society. You are a TERRORIST to blame God as the one who made you the way you are, a killer, a robber, an adulterer, a fornicator, a prostitute, etc.

. . . .

- If the Ten Commandments were abolished at Calvary OR even just   one commandment   , then the death of JESUS at Calvary becomes null and void.

  - Therefore, sin would have become immortalized and mankind would have found an excuse to sin forever while professing to believe in JESUS as the Savior.
- And their claim to overcome temptations by the blood of JESUS is all in vain around an idol golden calf.
  - Matthew 5:17   -19; John 14:15; 1 John 2:3   -6; 3:4 -9; Revelation 14:12; 22:14.

CHAPTER 4

JESUS AS A HUMAN BEING KEPT THE TEN COMMANDMENTS.

SCRIPTURE: Hebrews 4:14-15.

[14] Seeing then that we have a great high priest, that is passed into the heavens, Jesus the Son of God, let us hold fast our profession.

[15] For we have not an high priest which cannot be touched with the feeling of our infirmities; <u>but was in all points tempted like as we are, yet without sin.</u>

· ·

1 Peter 2:21-22

[21] <u>For even hereunto were ye called: because Christ also suffered for us, leaving us an example, that ye should follow his steps:</u>

[22] <u>Who did no sin, neither was guile found in his mouth:</u>

· ·

EXPLANATION

Jesus while on earth as a human being was tempted in all things as we are, yet never sinned.

He did not transgress the law. He kept the law perfectly. He kept the Sabbath day holy – (Luke 4:16). Jesus is our example that a born - again Christian can keep God's law. Therefore, sin is no excuse.

When you are against the Ten Commandments, you are against JESUS who wrote the Ten Commandments and gave through Moses at Mount Sinai.

No person can keep the law of God without the power of God. That is the reason you and I must be born-again Christians to be able to keep God's law- (1 John 3:6-9). It is the power of God that can help us keep God's law. Let's read the Scripture given below.

1 John 3:6-9 (KJV).

[6] <u>Whosoever abideth in him sinneth not</u>: whosoever sinneth hath not seen him, neither known him.

[7] Little children, let no man deceive you: he that doeth righteousness is righteous, even as he is righteous.

[8] <u>He that committeth sin is of the devil</u>; for the devil sinneth from the beginning. For this purpose the Son of God was manifested, that he might destroy the works of the devil.

[9] <u>Whosoever is born of God doth not commit sin; for his seed remaineth in him: and he cannot sin, because he is born of God.</u>

. . . .

Therefore, the Ten Commandments can be kept. Jesus did not come to change the Ten Commandments. He came to prove that the Ten Commandments can be kept – (Matthew 5:17-19).

The belief that the Ten Commandments cannot be kept is a Satanic belief to degrade the atonement of JESUS at Calvary and to make the sacrifice of JESUS null and void.

It is a belief to attack the authority of God which is found in his law.

THINK ABOUT THIS: Any government on earth that does not have any laws to convict criminals will be in chaos.

So, remember this. God's government has the moral law. When one third of the angels transgressed the law in heaven, they we cast out to our planet earth before Adam and Eve were created. And when Adam and Eve transgressed God's law, they were cast out from the Garden of Eden. They were not allowed to eat of the tree of the knowledge of good and evil to avoid them becoming immortal sinners. And the tree of life was removed from them.

He or she that transgresseth the law is of the devil – (1 John 3:8). But he or she that is born of God cannot transgress the law. Because God lives in him and her.

No sin of Adam and Eve was transferred to Cain and Abel nor to a baby. Jesus was the Sin Bearer for Adam and Eve – (John 1:29; 2 Corinthians 5:21; Ezekiel 18:20).

. . . .

CHAPTER 5

FAITH WITHOUT WORKS IS DEAD.

SCRIPTURE

James 2:17-25(KJV).

¹⁷ Even so faith, if it hath not works, <u>is dead, being alone.</u>

¹⁸ Yea, a man may say, Thou hast faith, and I have works: shew me thy faith without thy works, and I will shew thee my faith by my works.

¹⁹ Thou believest that there is one God; thou doest well: the devils also believe, and tremble.

²⁰ <u>But wilt thou know, O vain man, that faith without works is dead?</u>

²¹ <u>Was not Abraham our father justified by works, when he had offered Isaac his son upon the altar?</u>

²² Seest thou how faith wrought with his works, and by works was faith made perfect?

²³ And the scripture was fulfilled which saith, <u>Abraham believed God, and it was imputed unto him for righteousness: and he was called the Friend of God.</u>

²⁴ <u>Ye see then how that by works a man is justified, and not by faith only.</u>

²⁵ Likewise also was not <u>Rahab</u> the harlot justified by works, when she had received the messengers, and had sent them out another way?

. . . .

EXPLANATION

According to the Scripture above (James 2:17-25), this is what is says:

1. Faith alone is dead.

2. Faith without obedience is dead.

3.   Faith must produce obedience then it is pleasing unto God.

4.   Faith and obedience go hand in hand.

5.   Faith is genuine when obedience is the fruit of faith.

6.   Obedience will always become the fruit of genuine faith.

7.   Obedience is <u>not </u>the fruit of salvation.

8.   Faith and Obedience must <u>precede</u> forgiveness and the gift of eternal life.

9.   The gift of forgiveness and eternal life will <u>not</u> be given to a sinner who continues to transgress the law of God.

10. Repentance from sin is the turning away from disobedience to obedience.

11. Genuine repentance leads a person to have faith in God's word, and obedience is the result <u>before</u> the gift of forgiveness and eternal life is granted by JESUS.

· ·

The above 11 points need to be understood well. If you failed to understand the 11 points stated above, then you would have a problem of not understanding James 2:17-25.

Abraham had a genuine faith and obeyed God when he took Isaac to sacrifice on Mount Moriah. This act of <u>faith and obedience</u> by Abraham was pleasing to God – (Genesis 22:15-18).

· ·

- **James 2:17-25(KJV).**
- **17 Even so faith, if it hath not works, is dead, being alone.**
- **18 Yea, a man may say, Thou hast faith, and I have works: shew me thy faith without thy works, and I will shew thee my faith by my works.**
- **19 Thou believest that there is one God; thou doest well: the devils also believe, and tremble.**
- **20 But wilt thou know, O vain man, that faith without works is dead?**
- **21 Was not Abraham our father justified by works, when he had offered Isaac his son upon the altar?**
- **22 Seest thou how faith wrought with his works, and by works was faith made perfect?**
- **23 And the scripture was fulfilled which saith, Abraham believed God, and it was imputed unto him for righteousness: and he was called the Friend of God.**
- **24 Ye see then how that by works a man is justified, and not by faith only.**
- **25 Likewise also was not Rahab the harlot justified by works, when she had received the messengers, and had sent them out another way?**

- Genesis 22:1-18
- 1. And it came to pass after these things, that God did tempt Abraham, and said unto him, Abraham: and he said, Behold, here I am
- [2] And he said, Take now thy son, thine only son Isaac, whom thou lovest, and get thee into the land of Moriah; and offer him there for a burnt offering upon one of the mountains which I will tell thee of.
- [3] And Abraham rose up early in the morning, and saddled his ass, and took two of his young men with him, and Isaac his son, and clave the wood for the burnt offering, and rose up, and went unto the place of which God had told him.
- [4] Then on the third day Abraham lifted up his eyes, and saw the place afar off.
- [5] And Abraham said unto his young men, Abide ye here with the ass; and I and the lad will go yonder and worship, and come again to you.
- [6] And Abraham took the wood of the burnt offering, and laid it upon Isaac his son; and he took the fire in his hand, and a knife; and they went both of them together.
- [7] And Isaac spake unto Abraham his father, and said, My father: and he said, Here am I, my son. And he said, Behold the fire and the wood: but where is the lamb for a burnt offering?
- [8] And Abraham said, My son, God will provide himself a lamb for a burnt offering: so they went both of them together.
- [9] And they came to the place which God had told him of; and Abraham built an altar there, and laid the wood in order, and bound Isaac his son, and laid him on the altar upon the wood.
- [10] And Abraham stretched forth his hand, and took the knife to slay his son.
- [11] And the angel of the LORD called unto him out of heaven, and said, Abraham, Abraham: and he said, Here am I.
- [12] And he said, Lay not thine hand upon the lad, neither do thou any thing unto him: for now I know that thou fearest God, seeing thou hast not withheld thy son, thine only son from me.
- [13] And Abraham lifted up his eyes, and looked, and behold behind him a ram caught in a thicket by his horns: and Abraham went and took the ram, and offered him up for a burnt offering in the stead of his son.
- [14] And Abraham called the name of that place Jehovahjireh: as it is said to this day, In the mount of the LORD it shall be seen.
- [15] And the angel of the LORD called unto Abraham out of heaven the second time,
- [16] And said, By myself have I sworn, saith the LORD, for because thou hast done this thing, and hast not withheld thy son, thine only son:
- [17] That in blessing I will bless thee, and in multiplying I will multiply thy seed as the stars of the heaven, and as the sand which is upon the sea shore; and thy seed shall possess the gate of his enemies;
- [18] And in thy seed shall all the nations of the earth be blessed; because thou hast obeyed my voice.

CHAPTER 6

THE SEVENTH DAY OF THE WEEK IS THE SABBATH.

SCRIPTURE:

Exodus 20:8-11 (KJV).

[8] Remember the sabbath day, to keep it holy.

[9] Six days shalt thou labour, and do all thy work:

[10] But the seventh day is the sabbath of the LORD thy God: in it thou shalt not do any work, thou, nor thy son, nor thy daughter, thy manservant, nor thy maidservant, nor thy cattle, nor thy stranger that is within thy gates:

[11] For in six days the LORD made heaven and earth, the sea, and all that in them is, and rested the seventh day: wherefore the LORD blessed the sabbath day, and hallowed it.

. . . .

EXPLANATION

The seventh day of the week is the Sabbath of the LORD who created Adam and Eve. In fact, the seventh day every week reminds us that God created heaven and earth in six days and rested on the seventh-day – (Genesis 1:31; 2:1-3).

Adam and Eve were not Jews when God gave them the seventh day to rest. The weekly Sabbath day is not a Jewish law nor the law of Moses.

God who created heaven and earth gave us the weekly cycle of seven days and marked the seventh day as the Sabbath to remind us that God is the Creator. Therefore, the teaching of evolution is against the Sabbath day of JESUS. And the teaching that says JESUS abolished the Sabbath Commandment after his death at Calvary is Satanic and is Anti-Christ.

Those who teach that the Ten Commandments were abolished at Calvary after the death of JESUS, they also teach that the Sabbath Commandment was changed from the seventh day to the first day of the week.

Their reasoning is based on Sunday as the day that JESUS resurrected. This kind of theology sounds good, but full of heresy. It is Anti-Christ and illogical.

In the New Testament, JESUS healed the sick on the Sabbath day as well as other days of the week. The healing of the sick on the Sabbath did not change the Sabbath day from Saturday to Sunday. It is lawful to do good on the Sabbath day.

The Jews in Jesus time tried to keep the Sabbath day holy but rejected Jesus as the Creator and law-giver. They are so contradicting.

Today, many Pastors preach JESUS as the Messiah but reject Him as the law-giver. JESUS is the same yesterday, today, and forever – (Hebrews 13:8). HE is the LORD OF THE SABBATH – (Mark 2:27-28).

. . . .

- **Exodus 20:8-11 (KJV).**
- **⁸ Remember the sabbath day, to keep it holy.**

- **⁹ Six days shalt thou labour, and do all thy work:**

- **¹⁰ But the seventh day is the sabbath of the LORD thy God: in it thou shalt not do any work, thou, nor thy son, nor thy daughter, thy manservant, nor thy maidservant, nor thy cattle, nor thy stranger that is within thy gates:**

- **¹¹ For in six days the LORD made heaven and earth, the sea, and all that in them is, and rested the seventh day: wherefore the LORD blessed the sabbath day, and hallowed it.**

. . . .

CHAPTER 7

THE TEN COMMANDMENTS CAN BE KEPT BY BORN AGAIN CHRISTIANS.

1 John 3:3-9 (KJV).

[3] And every man that hath this hope in him purifieth himself, even as he is pure.

[4] Whosoever committeth sin transgresseth also the law: for sin is the transgression of the law.

[5] And ye know that he was manifested to take away our sins; and in him is no sin.

[6] <u>Whosoever abideth in him sinneth not: whosoever sinneth hath not seen him, neither known him.</u>

[7] Little children, let no man deceive you: he that doeth righteousness is righteous, even as he is righteous.

[8] <u>He that committeth sin is of the devil</u>; for the devil sinneth from the beginning. For this purpose the Son of God was manifested, that he might destroy the works of the devil.

[9] <u>Whosoever is born of God doth not commit sin; for his seed remaineth in him: and he cannot sin, because he is born of God.</u>

. . . .

THE LAW CAN BE KEPT BY BORN AGAIN CHRISTIANS.

- 1 John 3:3-9 (KJV).
- [3] And every man that hath this hope in him purifieth himself, even as he is pure.
- [4] Whosoever committeth sin transgresseth also the law: for sin is the transgression of the law.
- [5] And ye know that he was manifested to take away our sins; and in him is no sin.
- [6] Whosoever abideth in him sinneth not: whosoever sinneth hath not seen him, neither known him.
- [7] Little children, let no man deceive you: he that doeth righteousness is righteous, even as he is righteous.
- [8] He that committeth sin is of the devil; for the devil sinneth from the beginning. For this purpose the Son of God was manifested, that he might destroy the works of the devil.
- [9] Whosoever is born of God doth not commit sin; for his seed remaineth in him: and he cannot sin, because he is born of God.

· ·

CHAPTER 8

GOD CREATED NO BABY SINNER(S) FROM ADAM.

Psalm 100:1-5 (KJV).

1. Make a joyful noise unto the Lord, all ye lands.

² Serve the Lord with gladness: come before his presence with singing.

³ Know ye that <u>the Lord he is God</u>: <u>it is he that hath made us</u>, and not we ourselves; we are his people, and the sheep of his pasture.

⁴ Enter into his gates with thanksgiving, and into his courts with praise: <u>be thankful unto him, and bless his name.</u>

⁵ <u>For the Lord is good; his mercy is everlasting; and his truth endureth to all generations.</u>

. . . .

God who created us in the mother's womb made no baby sinner, no murderer, no prostitute, no fornicator, no idol worshiper, etc. He created sinless babies. We were all created in the image of God, a sinless baby.

The belief that says, "we were born sinners because of Adam's sin in us," is a Satanic doctrine to immortalize sin through every born. This false doctrine is Anti-Christ and must be confronted, condemned, and rebuked. We must not spare the rod but condemn it.

This false doctrine is against the gospel of JESUS to make his atonement at Calvary null and void.

CHAPTER 9

THE FALSE DOCTRINE THAT ABOLISHED GOD'S 10 COMMANDMENTS.

The teaching that says "sin is by nature due to the sinful nature we inherited from Adam" is a Satanic teaching to abolish the Ten Commandments of God. How? It is attacking the definition of sin recorded in 1 John 3:4.

THE TRUTH IS: We inherited the fallen sinful nature from Adam. But we did not inherit sin. Inheriting the fallen sinful nature and inheriting sin are two different things. Unfortunately, most people and Pastors don't know the difference because they have been brainwashed by a man-made doctrine.

· ·

FACT # 1: One third of the angels in heaven transgressed the law and were cast out of heaven. When they sinned, they did not have a fallen sinful nature. Therefore, sin is not by the fallen sinful nature. Sin cannot be defined by a fallen sinful nature.

FACT # 2: Adam and Eve transgressed the law of God at the Garden of Eden without a fallen sinful nature. Therefore, sin is not by the fallen sinful nature. . . . The fallen sinful nature is the *result* of sin. The fallen sinful nature is not the cause of sin. Cause and Effect (Result) are two different things.

Surely, we must learn to reason and use common sense.

· ·

WHICH COMMANDMENT IN THE TEN COMMANDMENTS THAT ADAM AND EVE TRANSGRESSED?

Adam and Eve transgressed the first commandment in the Ten Commandments. They chose to believe in Satan's lie. Therefore, they broke the first Commandment where God says, "Thou shalt have no other gods before Me." They chose Satan who spoke through the serpent to be their god.

Adam and Eve also transgressed the 10th Commandment. They coveted and ate the tree of the knowledge of good and evil which does not belong to them.

They manifested <u>no faith</u> in God. Their lack of faith led them to disobey God's commandments.

. . . .

- THE TRUTH
- 1 John 3:4   – "Sin is the transgression of the law."

- THE ERROR
- Sin is by the fallen sinful nature.

CHAPTER 10

BY FAITH ABRAHAM OBEYED GOD.

SCRIPTURE:

Hebrews 11:4-8 – (KJV).

[4] <u>By faith Abel offered unto God a more excellent sacrifice than Cain,</u> by which he obtained witness that he was righteous, God testifying of his gifts: and by it he being dead yet speaketh.

[5] <u>By faith Enoch was translated that he should not see death;</u> and was not found, because <u>God had translated him:</u> for before his translation he had this testimony, that <u>he pleased God.</u>

[6] <u>But without faith it is impossible to please him: for he that cometh to God must believe that he is, and that he is a rewarder of them that diligently seek him.</u>

[7] <u>By faith Noah, being warned of God of things not seen as yet, moved with fear, prepared an ark to the saving of his house; by the which he condemned the world, and became heir of the righteousness which is by faith.</u>

[8] <u>By faith Abraham, when he was called to go out into a place which he should after receive for an inheritance, obeyed; and he went out, not knowing whither he went.</u>

. . . .

1. CAIN TRANSGRESSED GOD'S LAW.

Cain did not have faith in God. And he disobeyed God. As a result, his sacrifice was not approved by God. Cain transgressed God's law.

. . . .

2. ABEL OBEYED GOD'S LAW.

Abel, the Son of Adam and Eve loved God and obeyed Him. As a result, God honored his sacrifice. But Cain who out of jealousy, hated his neighbor and killed his brother Abel.

Abel became the first martyr in the name of JESUS. Though Abel was dead due to Cains hatred, yet will be resurrected by JESUS when He returns again to take the righteous to heaven – (1 Thessalonians 4:16-17).

. . . .

3. ENOCH OBEYED GOD'S LAW.

Enoch who lived before the flood truly loved God and obeyed His Commandments. As a result, God translated Enoch and took to heaven.

. . . .

4. NOAH OBEYED GOD'S LAW.

Noah was called by God to build an Ark according to the instructions because there will be a flood. And Noah faithfully did as God asked him to do – (Genesis 6 and 7).

The world had not yet seen rain before, and Noah believed in what God said and did exactly as was told. Noah did not only build the Ark, but faithfully preached for 120 years that there will be a flood. The Ark was meant to be the place of refuge during the flood for those who believed in Noah's message from God.

Unfortunately, only Noah and his family by faith believed God and entered the Ark. They (8 people) were the only ones that did not die during the flood. Noah and his wife, and their three sons and their three wives were saved in the Ark. A great lesson for us to learn of faith and obedience. You cannot separate genuine faith from obedience.

Noah became the heir of righteousness by faith – (Hebrews 11:7).

. . . .

5. ABRAHAM OBEYED GOD'S LAW.

Abraham is another character in the Bible that we need to learn of his faith and obedience to God.

When God called upon Abraham to leave his country and go to a place where God will show him, and by faith Abraham obeyed and left yet he did not know where he was going to – (Genesis 12:1-4).

At his old age at 75, Abraham did not have a child. God promised to give him a Son. Sarah was old too.

Abraham and Sarah lacked the faith that God would give them a son through them. They opted to have the child from Hagar, the Egyptian house maid. But they later learned of their mistake, repented and returned to God. And God gave Isaac at their old age. Abraham was 100 years and Sarah was 90 years when Isaac was born. Amen.

Genesis 18:12-14

[12] Therefore Sarah laughed within herself, saying, After I am waxed old shall I have pleasure, my lord being old also?

[13] And the LORD said unto Abraham, Wherefore did Sarah laugh, saying, Shall I of a surety bear a child, which am old?

[14] <u>Is any thing too hard for the LORD? At the time appointed I will return unto thee, according to the time of life, and Sarah shall have a son.</u>

. . . .

Genesis 22:18

[18] And in thy seed shall all the nations of the earth be blessed; <u>because thou hast obeyed my voice.</u>

. . . .

- Genesis 22:118
- 1. And it came to pass after these things, that God did tempt Abraham, and said unto him, Abraham: and he said, Behold, here I a
- [2] And he said, Take now thy son, thine only son Isaac, whom thou lovest, and get thee into the land of Moriah; and offer him there for a burnt offering upon one of the mountains which I will tell thee of.
- [3] And Abraham rose up early in the morning, and saddled his ass, and took two of his young men with him, and Isaac his son, and clave the wood for the burnt offering, and rose up, and went unto the place of which God had told him.
- [4] Then on the third day Abraham lifted up his eyes, and saw the place afar off.
- [5] And Abraham said unto his young men, Abide ye here with the ass; and I and the lad will go yonder and worship, and come again to you.
- [6] And Abraham took the wood of the burnt offering, and laid it upon Isaac his son; and he took the fire in his hand, and a knife; and they went both of them together.
- [7] And Isaac spake unto Abraham his father, and said, My father: and he said, Here am I, my son. And he said, Behold the fire and the wood: but where is the lamb for a burnt offering?
- [8] And Abraham said, My son, God will provide himself a lamb for a burnt offering: so they went both of them together.
- [9] And they came to the place which God had told him of; and Abraham built an altar there, and laid the wood in order, and bound Isaac his son, and laid him on the altar upon the wood.
- [10] And Abraham stretched forth his hand, and took the knife to slay his son.
- [11] And the angel of the LORD called unto him out of heaven, and said, Abraham, Abraham: and he said, Here am I.
- [12] And he said, Lay not thine hand upon the lad, neither do thou any thing unto him: for now I know that thou fearest God, seeing thou hast not withheld thy son, thine only son from me.
- [13] And Abraham lifted up his eyes, and looked, and behold behind him a ram caught in a thicket by his horns: and Abraham went and took the ram, and offered him up for a burnt offering in the stead of his son.
- [14] And Abraham called the name of that place Jehovahjireh: as it is said to this day, In the mount of the LORD it shall be seen.
- [15] And the angel of the LORD called unto Abraham out of heaven the second time,
- [16] And said, By myself have I sworn, saith the LORD, for because thou hast done this thing, and hast not withheld thy son, thine only son:
- [17] That in blessing I will bless thee, and in multiplying I will multiply thy seed as the stars of the heaven, and as the sand which is upon the sea shore; and thy seed shall possess the gate of his enemies;
- [18] And in thy seed shall all the nations of the earth be blessed; because thou hast obeyed my voice.

CHAPTER 11

DELIVERANCE FROM EGYPT IS NOT WITHOUT OBEDIENCE – (PASSOVER).

. . . .

Scripture: Exodus 12:1-14 (KJV).

12 And the LORD spake unto Moses and Aaron in the land of Egypt saying,

[2] This month shall be unto you the beginning of months: it shall be the first month of the year to you.

[3] Speak ye unto all the congregation of Israel, saying, In the tenth day of this month they shall take to them every man a lamb, according to the house of their fathers, a lamb for an house:

[4] And if the household be too little for the lamb, let him and his neighbour next unto his house take it according to the number of the souls; every man according to his eating shall make your count for the lamb.

[5] Your lamb shall be without blemish, a male of the first year: ye shall take it out from the sheep, or from the goats:

[6] And ye shall keep it up until the fourteenth day of the same month: and the whole assembly of the congregation of Israel shall kill it in the evening.

[7] And they shall take of the blood, and strike it on the two side posts and on the upper door post of the houses, wherein they shall eat it.

[8] And they shall eat the flesh in that night, roast with fire, and unleavened bread; and with bitter herbs they shall eat it.

[9] Eat not of it raw, nor sodden at all with water, but roast with fire; his head with his legs, and with the purtenance thereof.

[10] And ye shall let nothing of it remain until the morning; and that which remaineth of it until the morning ye shall burn with fire.

[11] And thus shall ye eat it; with your loins girded, your shoes on your feet, and your staff in your hand; and ye shall eat it in haste: it is the LORD's passover.

[12] For I will pass through the land of Egypt this night, and will smite all the firstborn in the land of Egypt, both man and beast; and against all the gods of Egypt I will execute judgment: I am the LORD.

[13] And the blood shall be to you for a token upon the houses where ye are: and when I see the blood, I will pass over you, and the plague shall not be upon you to destroy you, when I smite the land of Egypt.

[14] And this day shall be unto you for a memorial; and ye shall keep it a feast to the LORD throughout your generations; ye shall keep it a feast by an ordinance for ever.

. . . .

EXPLANATION

Before the children of Israel left Egypt, the instruction was given that the blood of the lamb is to be painted on the door post. Any house that does not have the blood on the door post, the first born will die when the angel passes at mid-night. This is called the PASSOVER NIGHT.

Faith in God led the people to believe and obey the commandment. The Passover feast is held on the 14th day of the month of Nisan. It is to remind the children of Israel every year that it was God who delivered them from slavery in Egypt. They were to celebrate this PASSOVER feast every year as a reminder to the children and descendants of Jacob (Israel).

Faith goes together with obedience. Obedience is the fruit of faith.

CHAPTER 12

THE RICH YOUNG RULER DID NOT OBEY THE LAW AS CLAIMED.

SCRIPTURE: Matthew 19:16-26 (KJV).

¹⁶ And, behold, one came and said unto him, Good Master, what good thing shall I do, that I may have eternal life?

¹⁷ And he said unto him, Why callest thou me good? there is none good but one, that is, God: but if thou wilt enter into life, keep the commandments.

¹⁸ He saith unto him, Which? Jesus said, Thou shalt do no murder, Thou shalt not commit adultery, Thou shalt not steal, Thou shalt not bear false witness,

¹⁹ Honour thy father and thy mother: and, Thou shalt love thy neighbour as thyself.

²⁰ The young man saith unto him, All these things have I kept from my youth up: what lack I yet?

²¹ Jesus said unto him, If thou wilt be perfect, go and sell that thou hast, and give to the poor, and thou shalt have treasure in heaven: and come and follow me.

²² But when the young man heard that saying, he went away sorrowful: for he had great possessions.

²³ Then said Jesus unto his disciples, Verily I say unto you, That a rich man shall hardly enter into the kingdom of heaven.

²⁴ And again I say unto you, It is easier for a camel to go through the eye of a needle, than for a rich man to enter into the kingdom of God.

²⁵ When his disciples heard it, they were exceedingly amazed, saying, Who then can be saved?

²⁶ But Jesus beheld them, and said unto them, With men this is impossible; but with God all things are possible.

. . . .

EXPLANATION –

1. The rich young ruler asked the most important question to JESUS – What good thing must I do to have eternal life?

2. JESUS gave a straight answer that none should be confused.

3. JESUS said, "Keep the Commandments." (Matthew 19:17).

4. JESUS quoted the Commandment to love your neighbor – it is to do with the last six commandments of the Ten Commandments – (Matthew 19:18-19).

5. The rich young ruler claimed that he kept the commandments since his young age – (Matthew 19:20).

6. Then JESUS said to the rich young ruler to go and sell his possessions and give to the poor.

7. The rich young ruler was sorrowful and proved that he did not keep the Commandments as he claimed to be. He did not love his neighbor. This also proves that he did not love God.

8. The rich young ruler failed to realize that JESUS who spoke to him was the Creator of heaven and earth who made him rich and can make him more rich if he went and do as JESUS asked him to do.

9. It also proved that the rich young ruler loved wealth more than the One who gave him the wealth.

10. Then JESUS said, It will be hard for a rich man to enter heaven – (Matthew 19:23).

11. JESUS did not say, All rich men will not enter heaven.

12. Abraham was a rich man, but he loved God more than wealth. He loved God the giver more than the gifts of God.

13. Job is another person who loved God more than the wealth gifts given by God to him.

CHAPTER 13

THE ADULTEROUS WOMAN – MARY MAGDALENE

Scripture:

John 8:1-12 (KJV).

8 Jesus went unto the mount of Olives.

² And early in the morning he came again into the temple, and all the people came unto him; and he sat down, and taught them.

³ And the scribes and Pharisees brought unto him a woman taken in adultery; and when they had set her in the midst,

⁴ They say unto him, Master, <u>this woman was taken in adultery, in the very act.</u>

⁵ Now Moses in the law commanded us, that such should be stoned: but what sayest thou?

⁶ This they said, tempting him, that they might have to accuse him. <u>But Jesus stooped down, and with his finger wrote on the ground, as though he heard them not.</u>

⁷ <u>So when they continued asking him, he lifted up himself, and said unto them, He that is without sin among you, let him first cast a stone at her.</u>

⁸ And again he stooped down, and wrote on the ground.

⁹ And they which heard it, being convicted by their own conscience, went out one by one, beginning at the eldest, even unto the last: and Jesus was left alone, and the woman standing in the midst.

¹⁰ <u>When Jesus had lifted up himself, and saw none but the woman, he said unto her, Woman, where are those thine accusers? hath no man condemned thee?</u>

¹¹ <u>She said, No man, Lord. And Jesus said unto her, Neither do I condemn thee: go, and sin no more.</u>

¹² Then spake Jesus again unto them, saying, <u>I am the light of the world: he that followeth me shall not walk in darkness, but shall have the light of life.</u>

· ·

EXPLANATION

The adulterous woman was caught in the act. Who she committed adultery with is not told in the Scriptures – (John 8:1-12) . . . . Both, male and female need to be stoned; not just Mary Magdalene.

According to the Jewish law, the community is to stone her and the male partner to death. Jesus called on those who found her in the act of adultery to stone her to death, if they had not sinned. Slowly the accusers disappeared and Jesus was left alone with Mary Magdalene. Jesus who never sinned had the right to stone her to death but he did not.

Jesus who is the Savior of the world extended grace to the adulterous woman. He did not forgive her in sin. But he said to her – "Go and sin no more."

This grace extended allowed the adulterous woman to have the opportunity to repent from sin.

Later in her life, she revealed her repentance and love toward JESUS. She brought the costly alabaster oil and anointed Jesus and washed his feet. She used her hair as the towel to wipe the feet of JESUS. This was an act of true repentance of the heart. God saw the heart of the adulterous woman. And JESUS also saw the heart of the Pharisees who are self-righteous.

· ·

CHAPTER 14

GOD'S REMNANT PEOPLE WILL OBEY GOD'S COMMANDMENTS.

Scripture:

Revelation 14:12 (KJV).

[12] Here is the patience of the saints: here are they that keep the commandments of God, and the faith of Jesus.

Revelation 22:14 (KJV).

[14] Blessed are they that <u>do</u> his commandments, <u>that they may have right to the tree of life, and may enter in through the gates into the city.</u>

· ·

TAKE NOTE:

Those who love God and by faith obey his commandments will have eternal life. They will have the right to eat of the tree of life. They will enter in through the gates into the holy city – the New Jerusalem.

Even though the Ten Commandments is not the Savior, however, we who professed to love JESUS must be willing to obey his commandments, then eternal life will be given.

JESUS and his Ten Commandments are inseparable.

· ·

The gift of eternal life will be granted by JESUS to those who love him and keep his Commandments.

To profess that you love JESUS and yet reject the Ten Commandments that he wrote at Mount Sinail is hypocrisy.

The Jews tried to keep God's Ten Commandments including the Sabbath law, but rejected JESUS as their Savior and Creator of heaven and earth. They did not believe that JESUS was the God of Abraham, Isaac, and Jacob.

GOD'S REMNANT PEOPLE WILL OBEY HIS TEN COMMANDMENTS.

- Scripture:

- Revelation 14:12 (KJV).

- [12] Here is the patience of the saints: here are they that keep the commandments of God, and the faith of Jesus.

-

- Revelation 22:14 (KJV).

- [14] Blessed are they that do his commandments, that they may have right to the tree of life, and may enter in through the gates into the city.

GOD'S REMNANT PEOPLE WILL OBEY HIS TEN COMMANDMENTS.

- **Scripture:**

- **1 John 2:3-6 (KJV).**

- ³ And hereby we do know that we know him, <u>if we keep his commandments</u>.

- ⁴ <u>He that saith, I know him, and keepeth not his commandments, is a liar, and the truth is not in him.</u>

- ⁵ But whoso keepeth his word, in him verily is the love of God perfected: hereby know we that we are in him.

- ⁶ <u>He that saith he abideth in him ought himself also so to walk, even as he walked.</u>

CHAPTER 15

JESUS IS THE SAVIOR, NOT THE TEN COMMANDMENTS.

Jesus who created heaven and earth is eternal. After Adam and Eve sinned, JESUS became the Sin Bearer for Adam and Eve – (Genesis 3:15). He was <u>the lamb</u> that taketh away the sins of the world – (John 1:29).

We cannot be saved by any other name except by the name called "JESUS CHRIST OF NAZARETH" – (Acts 4:12; 2 Corinthians 5:21).

Adam and Eve's sins were transferred to JESUS. HE alone was the Sin Bearer for Adam and Eve. Their sins were not transferred to Cain nor to Abel nor to any baby that is born to this earth. This truth must be understood to counteract the false teachings of man.

The Ten Commandments is not the Savior. JESUS is the Savior. Even though the Ten Commandments is not the Savior, however, man cannot be given the gift of eternal life by JESUS if man continues to transgress God's law.

The sinner who professes to believe and have faith in JESUS must repent from transgressing God's law, then the gift of eternal life will be assured. Man may die but there is life after death when JESUS returns to take the saints to heaven – (Thessalonians 4:16-17; 1 Corinthians 15:52-55).

Be assured that death is not the end of life. We inherited <u>the first death</u> from Adam due to the consequences of his sin. <u>But the first death not the result of your sin.</u> The first death is only a temporary sleep. Those who died in the LORD will be resurrected to eternal life.

If JESUS did not resurrect from the grave, then our hope and faith in eternal life after death is in vain.

Because JESUS is alive and he lives, therefore, we can be resurrected from the grave when He comes again. Amen!

Belonging to a denomination which claims to be God's remnant Church does not guarantee you the gift of eternal life nor a remnant member of God's church on earth.

There a millions of people that believed that their denomination is God's remnant Church and they are the remnant of God because they are baptized members of that church. They have been deceived by their own Church and by their own Pastors.

God's Remnant Church is not a denomination. JESUS is not coming back to take a denomination but individuals who loved Him and by faith kept His Commandments.

God alone knows who the remnant are. Having your name after baptism on the denominations' church books does not make you a remnant member of God's church. Period!

· ·

> •JESUS IS THE SAVIOR. THE TEN COMMANDMENTS IS NOT THE SAVIOR. HOWEVER, A SINNER CANNOT BE GIVEN THE GIFT OF ETERNAL LIFE IF HE OR SHE CONTINUES TO TRANSGRESS GOD'S TEN COMMANDMENTS.

CHAPTER 16

JESUS ABOLISHED NOT ONE COMMANDMENT AT CALVARY.

The day JESUS died (Friday) around 3 pm in the afternoon, the curtain that separated the holy from the most holy apartment of the temple in Jerusalem was torn from top to bottom.

That signified the <u>end of animal sacrificial offerings</u>. JESUS became the real lamb that taketh away the sins of the world – (John 1:29). His death did not abolish the Ten Commandments. O yea, the death of JESUS did not abolish the Sabbath commandment either.

Let's be very clear. The death of Jesus did not abolish the Sabbath Commandment nor changed the Sabbath day from Saturday to Sunday.

The weekly Sabbath comes <u>52 times in a year.</u> But the resurrection day which is Sunday is celebrated <u>once a year</u> during the Easter week-end. Most people still don't know the difference between the weekly Sabbath in the Ten Commandments and the resurrection day.

• •

- IF the Ten Commandments were abolished at Calvary, then the death of JESUS at Calvary becomes null and void.

- Therefore, sin would have become immortalized and mankind would have had an excuse to commit sin forever while professing to believe in JESUS as the Savior. And their claim to overcome sin by the blood of JESUS is all in vain around an idol golden calf.

- IF the Ten Commandments were to be abolished, then they should have been abolished after Adam and Eve sinned at the Garden of Eden before Cain and Abel were born. And there would have been no need for the innocent LAMB to be killed as an atonement for their sin.

- And the Creator does not have to become the Sin Bearer nor become incarnated into human flesh through Mary at Bethlehem to die at Calvary.

- The incarnation of the Creator into human flesh and his (Jesus') death at Calvary is a proof that not even one commandment was changed nor abolished at Calvary.

- The death of JESUS at Calvary affirms that the Ten Commandments cannot be changed nor be abolished.

- The belief that says, When JESUS died at Calvary, he abolished the Ten Commandments. Thus, the Sabbath Commandment is no longer the seventh day of the week, but the first day of the week, is a Satanic doctrine to attack the authority of the law-giver which is JESUS who said, "IF you love me, keep my commandments" – (John 14:15).

CONCLUSION

The belief that says JESUS abolished the Ten Commandments at Calvary is a HOAX and must be confronted, rebuked, and condemned, to stop making the gospel null and void.

JESUS who was the YAHWEH who created our planet earth in six days and rested on the seventh day did <u>not</u> abolish one commandment at Calvary. HE who made us wrote the Ten Commandments on two tablets of stone and gave through Moses on Mount Sinai. He later came as a human being like us through Mary at Bethlehem to fulfill the law. HE kept the law perfectly and sinned not – (Hebrews 4:15). Therefore, sin is not excusable.

HE who wrote the law said, "IF you love me, keep my commandments." (John 14:15). HE did not come to change the law. Why should JESUS tell us to keep His law if the law cannot be kept?

It is illogical to think that JESUS changed the Ten Commandments after his death at Calvary. JESUS did <u>not</u> change the Ten Commandments before his death nor after his death.

IF the law was to be changed, then it should have been changed immediately after Adam and Eve's sin. And there would be no need for JESUS to become human flesh and die at Calvary.

Therefore, the death of JESUS at Calvary affirms that not one Commandment in the Ten Commandments was changed. The Ten Commandments are holy, righteous, and eternal - (Romans 7:12). God is eternal. Thus, his law is eternal.

HAVE YOU GIVEN A SERIOUS THOUGHT TO THIS?

• IF the law was to be changed, then it should have been changed immediately after Adam and Eve's sin at the Garden of Eden. And there would be no need for JESUS to become human flesh and die at Calvary.

• Therefore, the death of JESUS at Calvary affirms that not one Commandment in the Ten Commandments was changed.

• The Sabbath Commandment is still Saturday, not Sunday. Of course, the Resurrection day is not the Sabbath day.

• The Ten Commandments are holy, righteous, and eternal (Romans 7:12).

• God is eternal. Thus, his law is eternal. And everyone will be judged by the Ten Commandments – (Ecclesiastes 13:13-14).

• If the Ten Commandments were abolished at Calvary OR even just   one commandment   , then the death of JESUS at Calvary becomes null and void.

• Therefore, sin would have become immortalized and mankind would have found an excuse to sin forever while professing to believe in JESUS as the Savior.

• And their claim to overcome temptations by the blood of JESUS is all in vain around an idol golden calf.

• Matthew 5:17   -19; John 14:15; 1 John 2:3   -6; 3:4-9; Revelation   14:12; 22:14.

• The AUTHOR of this post: Metusela   F. Albert

JESUS WROTE THE TEN (10) COMMANDMENTS.

(HE ABOLISHED NONE AT CALVARY)

. . . .

METUSELA F. ALBERT

I am the author of these three Books:
Book # 1. 15 Reasons Why Babies Aren't Born Sinners.
Book # 2. JESUS was the Almighty God of Abraham. HE alone created heaven and earth.
Book # 3. JESUS wrote the Ten Commandments. He abolished none at Calvary.

Printed in the United States
By Bookmasters